HURRICANES

BY PETER MURRAY

Published by The Child's World®
1980 Lookout Drive • Mankato, MN 56003-1705
800-599-READ • www.childsworld.com

ACKNOWLEDGMENTS
The Child's World®: Mary Berendes, Publishing Director
Olivia Gregory: Editing

PHOTO CREDITS
© Carolyn Cole/Los Angeles Times: 17; Glynnis Jones/
Shutterstock.com: 15; lisafx/BigStock.com: 21; Lisa F. Young/
Shutterstock.com: 18; Matt Trommer/Shutterstock.com: 5;
NASA/NOAA: 7; razlomov/Shutterstock.com: 10; Sixty7a/
Dreamstime.com: 9; WeatherUnderground.com: 13; Zacarias
Pereira da Mata/Shutterstock.com: cover, 1

ISBN 9781631437670
LCCN 2014945416

Printed in the United States of America
Mankato, MN
November, 2014
PA02245

ABOUT THE AUTHOR

Peter Murray has written more than 80 children's books on science, nature, history, and other topics. He also writes novels for adults and teens under the name Pete Hautman. An animal lover, Peter lives in Golden Valley, Minnesota, in a house with one woman, two poodles, several dozen spiders, thousands of microscopic dust mites, and an occasional mouse.

Table of Contents

Swirling Clouds

Hurricanes are also called "cyclones" or "typhoons."

The National Hurricane Center is located in Miami, Florida. Scientists there study and track weather in hurricane areas.

The word "hurricane" comes from a Native American word meaning "evil spirit of the wind."

It is a hot, calm August day in Florida. But in outer space, a weather **satellite** detects something strange over the Atlantic Ocean. Some clouds are circling around, forming an enormous pinwheel hundreds of miles across. Using photos and information from the satellite, weather scientists called **meteorologists** learn a little more about the storm. They give the area of swirling clouds a name—it is now a **tropical storm**.

From outer space it's easy to see how a tropical storm swirls.

Hurricane Hunters

Hurricanes are given names to tell them apart. Up until 1979, only women's names were used.

If a hurricane does a lot of damage, its name is retired and it is never used again.

Each Hurricane Hunter flight lasts about 10 hours.

To learn more about strong storms, meteorologists use an airplane called a "Hurricane Hunter." This airplane is designed to fly in the roughest weather. The Hurricane Hunter flies directly into a storm's clouds. The plane's instruments measure the size, speed, direction, and force of the swirling clouds. The Hurricane Hunter sends its findings back to meteorologists.

If the meteorologists discover that a storm's winds are over 74 miles (119 km) per hour, they change the storm's name—they now call it a hurricane.

When this happens, meteorologists send out a **hurricane watch** for the areas where they expect the storm to hit. A hurricane watch means that a hurricane has formed over the ocean. There is a chance that the storm will reach the watch area within two days. People should be on alert and make plans in case the storm is dangerous.

This photo shows the Hurricane Hunter named Kermit. *The bubble on its belly is the radar system. The pole on the nose gathers information about wind gusts.*

Rating Hurricanes

Hurricanes are huge storms. They can be up to 600 miles (966 km) across.

Hurricanes in our part of the world always swirl counter-clockwise.

Hurricanes are the only type of weather disasters that are given their own names.

Scientists who study hurricanes rate them with a category system. Category 1 hurricanes are the weakest. They have winds of 74 to 95 miles (119 to 153 km) per hour. That's enough to blow the leaves off trees.

Category 5 hurricanes are the most powerful. They have winds over 155 miles (249 km) per hour. That's strong enough to tear up trees by their roots and bend lampposts to the ground!

Hurricane Gustav was a Category 4 hurricane that hit Louisiana in 2008. Its winds reached 155 miles (249 km) per hour. The storm caused over $2 billion in damage.

Warm–Weather Storms

Hurricanes form mostly during the warmer months of the year. During warm weather, the sun heats the ocean's surface all day long. Some of the water changes into a mist called **water vapor**. The warm water vapor rises high into the air. As it does, cooler air rushes in to replace it. This causes winds to form.

When conditions are right, the rising water vapor forms into clouds. The winds swirl the clouds into a huge doughnut shape hundreds of miles across. The clouds on the outside of the "doughnut" bring strong winds and very heavy rains. But the middle of the hurricane is peaceful.

The middle of a hurricane is called the **eye**. In the eye, the winds are calm and the weather is quiet. In fact, if you were in the eye of a hurricane, you could look straight up and see blue sky!

Hurricane season in the United States is between June 1 and November 30.

Hurricanes only form over water that is 80°F (27°C) or warmer.

Hurricanes are easiest to see from outer space. Here you can clearly see this storm's eye.

Hurricane Warning

As a hurricane gets closer to an area, meteorologists use computers to map the path of the storm and try to figure out where it will go. Sometimes scientists can tell exactly where a hurricane will go. Other times, the storm fools everyone and changes direction.

If meteorologists are sure a hurricane will reach an area within 24 hours, they issue a **hurricane warning**. This warning tells people to leave the area until the storm is over.

Meteorologists used maps to track where they believed Hurricane Gonzalo would travel in 2014. They also studied how strong the storm would be on certain days.

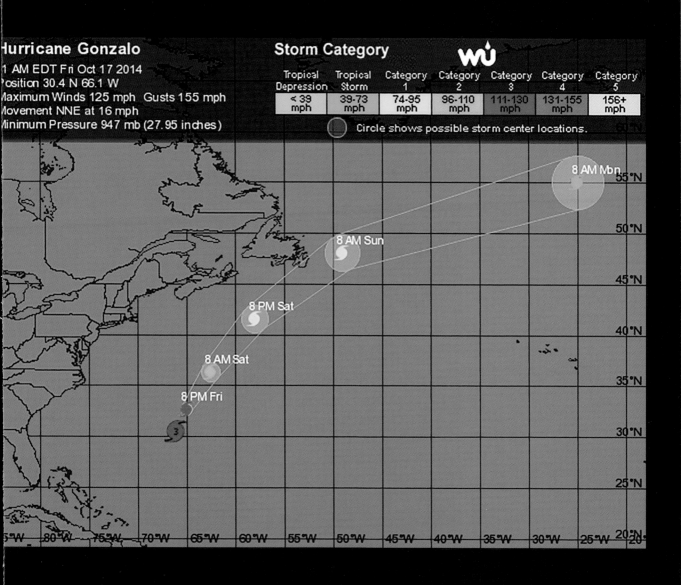

Hurricane Gonzalo

1 AM EDT Fri Oct 17 2014
Position 30.4 N 66.1 W
Maximum Winds 125 mph Gusts 155 mph
Movement NNE at 16 mph
Minimum Pressure 947 mb (27.95 inches)

Storm Category

wu

Tropical Depression	Tropical Storm	Category 1	Category 2	Category 3	Category 4	Category 5
< 39 mph	39-73 mph	74-95 mph	96-110 mph	111-130 mph	131-155 mph	156+ mph

Circle shows possible storm center locations.

8 AM Mon

8 AM Sun

8 PM Sat

8 AM Sat

8 PM Fri

3

Landfall!

When a hurricane reaches land, it's called "making landfall."

Hurricane Katrina had a storm surge of more than 25 feet (8 m).

The depth and power of a storm surge depends on many different things. The shape of an area's coastline and the power of the hurricane are two important parts.

As a hurricane approaches land, the sky grows very dark. Rain begins to fall, and the winds pick up. The wind might blow so hard that raindrops go sideways! Tree branches and roof shingles might tumble through the air. Sewers often back up, flooding the streets.

But the worst hurricane damage isn't caused by the wind and rain. The strong **storm surge** is the most dangerous part. As a hurricane nears land, the wind pushes a mound of water ahead of the storm. This raises the level of the ocean as much as 20 feet (6 m). The huge wall of water moves quickly toward land. When it finally crashes onto the shore, it destroys everything in its path. Imagine a wall of water as high as your house!

As it moves inland, a hurricane loses its power. Without the warm waters of the ocean to create its swirling winds, the storm calms down. In only a few hours, a hurricane is often just another rainstorm.

This roller coaster in New Jersey was destroyed by Hurricane Sandy in 2012. You can see how the storm surge flooded the area.

Hurricane Katrina

While New Orleans suffered the most damage during Katrina, the states of Mississippi and Alabama also had major damage.

Katrina was a Category 3 hurricane when it made landfall. Winds measured about 125 mph (201 kph).

Hurricane Katrina caused $108 billion in damage.

One of the worst hurricanes to hit the United States happened in 2005. Hurricane Katrina started as a tropical storm over the Bahamas on August 23. Within two days, meteorologists were warning the people of the United States' Gulf Coast that the storm was coming that way. Early on the morning of August 29, Hurricane Katrina made landfall near the border of Louisiana and Mississippi.

The city of New Orleans was one of the hardest hit areas. Winds completely destroyed buildings, businesses, and homes. The city flooded from the storm surge, and then **levees** broke. People scrambled to their attics and rooftops to escape the high waters. By the time the storm moved inland, more than 1,800 people had died.

After Katrina, the northern parts of New Orleans (the areas closest to Lake Pontchartrain) had some of the worst flooding.

Staying Safe

If there is a hurricane warning for the area where you live, you should take it very seriously. Board up all the windows in your home to keep them from breaking. Bring your lawn furniture and yard toys inside so they don't blow away in the strong winds. Most important, you and your family should get in your car and drive inland to wait out the storm.

It's a good idea to have a hurricane kit in your car. It should include things such as a first-aid kit, bottled water, a flashlight, and a battery-operated radio.

Stay indoors during a hurricane. That way, you are less likely to be hit by things being tossed around by the strong winds.

These men are putting boards over some windows before a hurricane hits.

Always Learning More

When a hurricane is over, stay away from flooded areas.

The planet Jupiter has had the same hurricane for more than 300 years. It looks like a giant red spot. The storm is larger than planet Earth!

Hurricanes are very dangerous storms. But even though we cannot stop them from happening, we can learn when and where they will strike. With the help of satellites, weather planes, computers, and meteorologists, we can understand more about these strong storms and how to protect ourselves from them.

Here you can see a meteorologist tracking a hurricane on his computer.

Glossary

eye (EYE)
The hole in the middle of a hurricane is called the eye. The weather in the eye is calm.

hurricane warning (HUR-uh-kayn WARN-ing)
A hurricane warning means that a hurricane will move into an area. The warning lets people know that they should leave the area until the storm is over.

hurricane watch (HUR-uh-kayn WATCH)
A hurricane watch means that there is a hurricane over the ocean. The watch tells people that the hurricane might move toward them.

levees (LEV-eez)
A levee is a wall of earth built up near a river to stop flooding.

meteorologists (mee-tee-yuh-ROL-uh-jists)
Meteorologists are scientists who study the weather. They try to predict where hurricanes will go.

satellite (SAT-uh-lyt)
A satellite is a machine that is sent into outer space to circle Earth. Some satellites help people learn about weather.

storm surge (STORM SURJ)
A storm surge is a huge wall of water pushed by a hurricane. Storm surges are dangerous and can cause lots of damage when they hit the shore.

tropical storm (TROP-ih-kull STORM)
A tropical storm is an area of swirling clouds, wind, and rain. If a tropical storm is strong enough, it becomes a hurricane.

water vapor (WA-tur VAY-pur)
When water gets heated, it turns into a mist called water vapor.

To Find Out More

In the Library

Challoner, Jack. *Hurricane & Tornado*. New York: DK Publishing, 2014.

Furgang, Kathy. *National Geographic Kids Everything Weather: Facts, Photos, and Fun that Will Blow You Away*. Washington, D.C.: National Geographic, 2012.

Rhodes, Jewell Parker. *Ninth Ward*. New York: Little, Brown and Co., 2012.

Tarshis, Lauren. *I Survived Hurricane Katrina, 2005*. New York: Scholastic, 2011.

On the Web

Visit our Web site for links about hurricanes:
www.childsworld.com/links

Note to Parents, Teachers, and Librarians: We routinely check our Web links to make sure they're safe, active sites—so encourage your readers to check them out!

Index